GREATEST FOOTBALL STARS

ACCESS THE ACTION!

Scan the QR code to
hear this story for

FREE!

Published in the UK by Sweet Cherry Publishing Limited, 2025
Unit 4u18, The Book Brothers Business Park, Tolwell Road,
Leicester LE4 1BR, United Kingdom

Sweet Cherry Publishing Limited
Unit 31, The Pottery, Bakers Point,
Pottery Road, Dún Laoghaire,
Dublin A96 EV18, Ireland

2 4 6 8 10 9 7 5 3

ISBN: 978-1-80263-544-7

Greatest Football Stars:
Peter Schmeichel

Text by Luke Paton
Illustrations by Sophie Jones

www.sweetcherrypublishing.com

Printed and bound in Turkey

MIX
Paper | Supporting responsible forestry
FSC® C111584
FSC www.fsc.org

Sweet Cherry

PETER SCHMEICHEL

THE UNOFFICIAL STORY

WRITTEN BY
LUKE PATON

CONTENTS

1

LEAGUE TROUBLE

On the 26th of May 1999, Manchester United were set to play against Bayern Munich in the Champions League final.

United had already won the Premier League and FA Cup, so they just needed to win the Champions League to secure a historic treble – an achievement no other English club had managed.

Peter Schmeichel, the team's captain for the match, led the United players out onto the pitch. It was his final game for the club, so he was determined to make it memorable. Throughout the competition, he had been a goalkeeping force to be reckoned with – and now it came down to one match. Could he help United achieve the treble?

Peter took a moment to think about everything they had achieved so far that season. Everything had gone their way. Surely it was destined to be their year?

But he knew Bayern Munich weren't interested in any of that. They had come here to win the trophy and were fighting for their own treble.

Six minutes into the match, Bayern got a free kick just outside the United area. Peter set up a four-man wall, carefully adjusting it left and right until it was perfect. He crouched and prepared for the shot.

Bayern was a clever side, and they added two of their own players to Peter's wall. Jaap Stam and Nicky Butt tried to push and jostle the Bayern players away, but it was no use. Suddenly, four more people were crowding Peter's wall and he couldn't see a thing. Just as Peter moved a step to his right to see the ball, Mario Basler took the shot. He whipped the ball in low and hard to Peter's left – precisely where he'd just been standing. It was in the back of the net before Peter even adjusted his feet.

Bayern were winning 1-0.

Peter smacked his hands together in disappointment. But he had to let it go. There was plenty more work for him to do.

The German side played immense football for the next forty-five minutes. Manchester United were on the back foot throughout. Peter had to keep his mind on the game. Anything could happen with this Bayern team. He watched a shot from Bayern's Alexander Zickler threaten the goal but go wide.

Let's get this to the break and regroup, thought Peter.

Sir Alex Ferguson, United's manager, gave the team an inspiring talk at half-time.

'At the end of this game, the European Cup will be six feet away,' he said, 'and you'll not even be able to touch it if we lose.'

The team talk fired up the United players – but Bayern still got the better of them after the restart.

One minute into the second half, Peter saved a shot from Carsten

Jancker. Then Basler tried to get the better of Peter again, with a David Beckham-like chip from near the halfway line. Fortunately, Peter watched that one fall over the bar.

Seventeen minutes from full time, Stefan Effenberg took a shot.

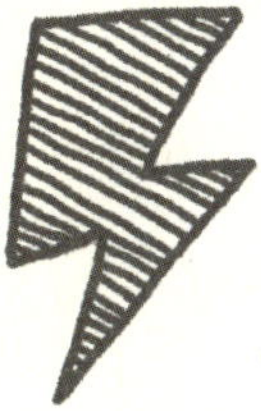

The ball blasted towards the goal. Peter used all his handball training to jump high and tip it harmlessly out for a corner. It was a crucial save.

But there was nothing Peter could do about Mehmet Scholl's perfectly weighted dink over him in the 79th minute. As soon as Scholl struck the ball, Peter thought it would go in. He jumped as high as he could, but he was nowhere near saving it. As Peter turned, he expected to see the ball drop into his net and put Bayern 2-0 up.

But it didn't. Somehow, the ball struck the post and rebounded into Peter's arms instead. He couldn't believe his luck!

If Manchester United equalised, they had a real chance of still winning the treble! Could they do it?

2

EARLY DAYS IN DENMARK

Peter Schmeichel was born on the 18th of November 1963. He fell in love with football at an early age and soon joined his local youth team in Denmark, Høje-Gladsaxe. His debut game came on the 7th of August 1972 (a day before his youngest sister was born!) when he was eight years old, and he played as a goalkeeper.

The goal was the best place for Peter to be. He wasn't great at controlling the ball with his feet, and he went a bit wild whenever he played in the outfield. Luckily, Peter was a natural between the posts!

'You'll end up playing for Denmark!' the grown-ups told him.

That was a lot of pressure for a young boy to live up to, but Peter put everything he had into the game. He practised with the team three days a week and played matches at the weekends. With Peter's help, Høje-Gladsaxe didn't lose a single game for two and a half years!

Thanks to this incredible run, Peter was able to play for a bigger and better team: BK Hero. Eventually, Hero merged with Gladsaxe to form Gladsaxe-Hero.

When Peter was seventeen years old, he was given the chance to join Gladsaxe-Hero's first team and play in the third division of the Danish league. People were starting to notice his amazing talent. The manager of Gladsaxe-Hero, Svend Aage Hansen, had a plan for him.

'You should be a part of this side,' he told Peter, 'but you should only stay with the club for two more seasons. Then you should make a move to Hvidovre's First Division side. After that, you will play for Denmark. Then you will have a professional career abroad.'

Peter was blown away! He hadn't been thinking about football as a real job at all ... but the idea of playing for Hvidovre in the First Division

(Denmark's top division at the time) was very exciting.

However, Gladsaxe-Hero didn't have a great season the next year and ended up one place above the relegation zone. To stay in the league, they had to win their final game of the season against Stubbekøbing ...

And they did! Peter was in top form and made lots of important saves.

When that final game ended, Hansen's daughter, Bente, ran out onto the pitch and gave Peter a big hug. That felt almost as good as not getting relegated! Peter fell in love with Bente at once and the pair quickly started dating. They got married in 1982 and went on to have two children together. Kasper arrived in 1986, and their daughter, Cecile, was born four years later.

In the years before Peter and Bente started their family, money was tight. Peter didn't earn very much while playing for Gladsaxe-Hero, and the pay wasn't much better when he moved to Hvidovre in 1984. He had to work all kinds of jobs and quickly became a jack of all trades. To make ends meet, Peter worked in a textile factory, in an office and as a cleaner at a care home. He even tried his hand at flooring!

So when Brøndby football club asked Peter to sign for them in 1987, he felt a sense of relief. Not only would he earn more money, but he could now call himself a professional footballer!

Brøndby was a good side, too. They won the First Division three times in Peter's first four seasons with the club. In the 1990/1991 season, the club hired a new manager, Morten Olsen, to take them to the next level.

Training under Olsen was brutal. In Olsen's first training session, he made Peter and the team drink champagne then go on a massive run for miles.

'I'm easing you in gently today,' he told the squad when they got back.

He wasn't kidding. Olsen wanted his team to be in peak physical condition when they competed during the season.

He focussed so much on making his side stronger that Peter sometimes didn't play a football match for two weeks!

'The players' legs are falling off!' the trainer warned Olsen.

Despite this, Olsen continued to push his team ... and it worked! When they did start playing again, they were better than ever. There were no teams in the Danish league who could stop them. In 1991, they won the league and their run in the UEFA Cup transformed Peter's life.

Olsen found all sorts of unique ways to motivate his team to win. Before they played Bayer Leverkusen in the third round of the UEFA Cup, Olsen pinned twenty 1,000-kroner notes (about £2,000) to the noticeboard. 'You're professionals!' he shouted at the players. 'Money is important to you! This is also what you're playing for tonight. If we go on to the next round, this is your bonus.'

It worked! The team won 3-0 that night and made it through to the quarter-finals. And they got the bonus!

Brøndby sneaked past Torpedo Moscow in the quarter-final, setting up an exciting semi-final against Roma. Unfortunately, a heartbreaking last-gasp goal from Roma's Rudi Völler knocked Brøndby out of the UEFA Cup.

Peter hated losing. He had hated it ever since he was a little boy. But in some ways, the UEFA Cup semi-final was the perfect last match for Peter at Brøndby. He played well and was noticed by scouts from outside of Denmark.

Peter was twenty-seven years old, and he thought it was time to move on. He wanted to move to England ... and a certain Premier League giant had their eye on him.

3

THE GREAT DANE

In 1991, Manchester United manager Alex Ferguson wanted a new goalkeeper. If he was going to have the greatest Reds side ever, he needed to sign the best of the best. He made it the mission of his goalkeeping coach, Alan Hodgkinson, to find him a strong and reliable keeper. Hodgkinson had heard good things about a goalie from Denmark called Peter Schmeichel, so he went to watch a match between Brøndby and Odense.

After just ten minutes, he knew he'd found the man Ferguson was looking for. Peter was six foot four, knew how to control his defence and had an unmistakeable presence in the goal. Hodgkinson thought he had the skills to be the best in the world.

Hodgkinson started to worry that another scout would swoop in and take Peter before he had the chance to talk to him. The moment the game ended, he got in touch with the bosses at Brøndby. They agreed to let Peter transfer to Manchester United.

'He's the one,' Hodgkinson told Ferguson on the phone. 'He will win the Premiership for you.'

'How much are they asking?' Ferguson asked.

'£500,000,' said Alan. 'Believe me, he'll be the bargain of the century.'

'Are you absolutely sure about the Schmeichel boy?'

'I am.'

'Can he play in the English game?'

'He will be an absolute certainty at Manchester United.'

Peter had other options that summer. Liverpool, Newcastle United, Queens Park Rangers and West Ham United had all shown an interest. But Peter had admired Manchester United since he was a child and the chance to play for them was a dream come true.

Peter arrived in Manchester later that summer. His family settled into the Ambelhurst Hotel, which was where they would be staying while Peter played football.

Luckily, Peter's kids loved the Ambelhurst Hotel. The place even had a playground! And even though the owner supported Manchester City, he made everyone feel very welcome.

Peter had a slightly rougher time settling into the United squad. The other players thought he was just another goalie who'd been bought for cheap from a club they'd never heard of. But Peter put them in their place right away!

On Peter's first day of training with the United lads, the assistant manager Brian Kidd started doing a drill called boxes, which is like piggy in the middle. In a small space, one team had to keep the ball away from the other team in as few touches as possible.

'Okay, we'll do boxes,' said Kidd. 'Peter, you can go with the other goalkeepers and do some half-volleys.'

'No, I'm in the boxes,' said Peter.

The other players were confused.

The goalkeepers never took part in boxes!

'I'm in the boxes,' Peter said again.

Kidd shrugged. From that day onwards, Peter was in the boxes. The squad then saw that Peter was in better shape than any other keeper.

Peter learnt all sorts of new skills under goalkeeping coach Alan Hodgkinson. Hodgkinson constantly reminded him that being a good goalkeeper was not just about making great saves. The most important thing was keeping the defence organised enough to stop the opposition from shooting at all.

Shouting at his defenders was always an important part of Peter's game. He liked to get himself locked into matches by directing the people in front of him.

'Left! Right!' he'd scream at them.

He did this even when he knew the defenders couldn't hear him!

This helped Peter concentrate on the match. It made him feel like he was part of the game even when the ball was nowhere near him.

It also helped to stop his mind from drifting. If he kept concentrating, it was less likely he'd make a mistake.

But one of the things Hodgkinson had to work on a lot with Peter was getting him to be a little bit easier on the players around him. Peter tended to tear into anyone who made a mistake. He had to learn that constant criticism wasn't always helpful and could negatively affect some players – particularly the younger ones in the team.

Of course, the other United players could give as good as they got. Peter had a love-hate relationship with defenders Steve Bruce and Gary Pallister.

Whenever Peter shouted at them during games, Bruce would often shout back: 'Get back in your goal!'

But they were all good friends off the pitch.

Another thing his team had to get used to was Peter's protectiveness about his goal. He didn't want the other players messing around or kicking the ball into his net. He didn't want them leaving towels or bibs or bottles in his net either. Peter hated anything going over his goal line! It was his job as the keeper to keep the goal empty – and that meant all the time.

His message was simple: 'Nothing gets in here today.'

Peter got off to a flying start in his first few matches. He even got the Man of the Match trophy in a pre-season game in Aberdeen.

He'd proved to his United teammates that he was a man they could rely on!

Peter had a few problems

getting used to the roughness of the English game. For example, an early match against Wimbledon left him quite shaken. The players barged into him and roughed him up every chance they got.

'Referee, referee!' Peter appealed, looking for help. But that was just how the game was played back then.

In another match against Leeds, Ferguson watched in horror as Peter missed a cross and let Lee Chapman score. *He's got no chance*, Ferguson thought.

Peter's official debut at Old Trafford was on the 17th of August 1991 against Notts County. The game drew a crowd of more than 46,000 people. Their cheers and chants gave Peter goosebumps. He'd never seen home team fans boost their side and help them to victory in such an amazing way.

It proved to be the perfect debut, with United winning 2-0. It was a sign of things to come, as the Reds only lost one match before Christmas 1991.

I have made the right decision about coming to Manchester, Peter thought.

He started to dream about reaching his ultimate goal: winning the First Division title (the same level as the Premier League today). To do this, he knew he had to always be at his best.

That's why Peter studied his performances after each match. He didn't ever allow himself to think he'd made a mistake. But he did look at goals and try to figure out if he could've done something differently.

The title race that year was extremely close. Manchester United kept Leeds

United at bay for most of the season, but then it all went wrong towards the end. The Reds had to play five games in two weeks, and the schedule was too much to cope with. In the end, Leeds pipped United to the post to finish five points ahead at the top of the table.

Peter had to be content with 'just' winning the League Cup (the first time United had ever won it) and the European Super Cup!

Even though the season ended with

some disappointment, Peter was in excellent form. He felt more than ready to join his Danish teammates in Sweden for a very special competition: Euro 1992.

It would be a summer he would never forget.

4

EURO '92

A year after making his debut for Denmark's first team in 1987, Peter became his country's first-choice goalkeeper.

Denmark was a good side, but they had a reputation for being a 'nearly' team. This meant they always nearly made it to the final before falling at the last hurdle.

It looked like Denmark was going to live up to this unflattering reputation in the summer of 1992 as well. The Euro 1992 championship was being held in Sweden, but Denmark had missed out on qualifying. They finished in second place in their group behind Yugoslavia.

However, Yugoslavia were disqualified from taking part just eleven days before the competition started. As runners up behind Yugoslavia, Denmark now had one more shot to make a name for themselves. Not that anybody believed they could win the trophy.

'Report tomorrow in Copenhagen,' the Danish first team were told. 'We've got a week to prepare.'

'We haven't got a chance,' the players moaned.

But manager Richard Møller Nielsen laid down the challenge in training. He brought his team together in the centre of the pitch. 'Let's make one thing clear,' he told them. 'We're going to Sweden to win the competition.'

The players started laughing – but Nielsen was deadly serious. Denmark's sudden entry into the competition put them in a strangely good position. After all, nobody thought they could win, so there was no pressure on them to perform.

Denmark's first group game was against England. England had reached the semi-final of the World Cup in 1990 and was one of the favourites to win the Euros. They expected to beat Denmark with ease.

But Peter and his Danish team put on a great performance. Peter kept a clean sheet, and his teammate John Faxe almost pinched them a winner – but his strike hit the post.

The game finished 0-0.

Denmark had heaps of confidence going into the next match against the hosts, Sweden.

Although Denmark played well, Sweden came out on top. Peter had to stay alert to constant danger throughout and the pressure finally got to him in the 58th minute. Sweden's Per Tomas Brolin got one goal past him, which was enough to win the match.

Peter was gutted, and so were the rest of the team. After the game, the Danish changing room was silent. The players assumed they now had no chance of going through to the next round.

The Euros were a little different back then compared to today. There were only two groups in the group stage, and the top two teams in each one went straight to the semi-finals. If Denmark wanted to go through in second place, they had to beat France in their final group game.

France had won every single one of their qualifying matches, and they'd drawn with both England and Sweden in their first Euro '92 group games. The French players were confident they were going all the way to the final.

In the tunnel before the game, the Danish and French players lined up next to one another. One of the French players came up to Denmark's John Sivebæk, who played club football in France at the time, and said, 'Don't be too tough on us today, don't be rough, because we've got to play the semi-final.'

Sivebæk translated the message for his teammates. 'No!' they responded. 'Absolutely no way are we going to let them off with that!'

Those comments fired up Denmark, and they went out to crush France's hopes of a European title. The Danish striker Henrik Larsson put them up 1-0 after just eight minutes!

Jean-Pierre Papin scored an equaliser for France before half-time, but Denmark's Lars Elstrup scored the winning goal twelve minutes from full time. Denmark were through to the semi-final!

It was an underdog story the press and the public couldn't resist. The team gained more and more fans with every game, but the manager tried to keep the atmosphere in the changing room calm and light. He let the players enjoy a round of crazy golf and even a trip to a fast food place before their big match.

In the semi-final, Denmark faced the Netherlands. The Dutch had won the previous Euros in 1988, and everyone expected them to win it

again. But the Danes had nothing to lose and weren't about to go down without a fight.

The match was a tight affair. Larsson put Denmark up 1-0 within five minutes, but Dennis Bergkamp levelled the score eighteen minutes later. Peter was very annoyed when Bergkamp squeezed in a goal underneath him as he dived.

Larsson scored again just before half-time and Denmark clung to that lead. Peter played well and cheered on his team ... but the Dutch were too good to stay behind for the rest of the game.

Frank Rijkaard equalised again for the Netherlands, so the game went into extra time and then penalties.

Penalty shoot-outs are always a nightmare for any team. Even though the players are shooting from only twelve yards out, there is a lot of pressure on them to score. Nobody wants to be the person who missed a penalty in an important shoot-out!

But when you're a goalie, like Peter, the situation is different. Nobody expects the goalkeeper to save a penalty. If they do manage to keep one out, they are instantly the heroes of the match.

Peter was actually looking forward to the penalty shoot-out against the Netherlands. He felt confident he could make a difference.

It's impossible for me to lose this, he thought.

Both teams scored their first penalties to make it 1-1. Then the Netherlands' Marco van Basten stepped up to take his kick.

Peter watched him place the ball on the penalty spot and decided which way he was going to dive. When van Basten ran and struck the ball, Peter didn't hesitate. He dived the way he had decided ... and saved the penalty!

It was the only missed penalty in the whole shoot-out, so Denmark went through to the final 5-4 on penalties!

The manager was full of praise for his team after the win – and he singled out Peter as 'that wonderful big mouse.'

Brian Laudrup, Peter's teammate, agreed that Peter was 'outstanding.'

But even though the Danes were enjoying this fairy tale run to the final, fans still thought they had no chance of winning it. Germany, their opponents in the final, had been strong throughout the competition.

Germany had won the World Cup in 1990, and their team was arguably even better in 1992 than it had been two years earlier. The nation and the players figured Denmark wouldn't be a problem for them.

Before the match, Germany's Stefan Effenburg asked Denmark's Laudrup if they could swap shirts after the game. He was obviously assuming the Germans were going to win!

'They think they just have to turn up here and pick up the gold medals!' Peter exclaimed. 'The French and Dutch had that attitude before they met us, and they lost. They were arrogant.'

Peter and the rest of the team wanted to prove them wrong. During the match, Peter made the most of his United training. He dominated from

the back and made many memorable saves.

He stopped Stefan Reuter from getting a clean shot on goal by rushing off his line and making himself as big as possible. His stretched-out arms got a vital touch on the ball to push it out for a corner.

Later, the legendary German striker Jürgen Klinsmann had a shot from outside the area that looked destined for the back of the net. But Peter got down low and finger-tipped it outside of the post.

That's one of the best saves of my career! thought Peter.

Peter's incredible shot-stopping allowed the strikers to do their thing at the other end of the pitch. In the 18th minute, Flemming Povlsen squared the ball for Faxe on the edge of the German penalty area. Faxe blasted the ball as hard as he could – and it slammed into the back of the net! It was 1-0 to Denmark!

Peter still had his work cut out for him. In the second half, Klinsmann got on the end of a cross with a powerful header. On any other day against any other keeper, it would have been a certain goal. But Peter was unbeatable that day! He got a strong hand on the ball and palmed it over the bar.

In the 77th minute, Germany began another attack. They approached the Danish byline and struck a high, looping cross into the area. Peter came off his line and jumped with outstretched arms. He caught the ball coolly with one hand!

One minute later, Denmark's Kim Vilfort attacked the German goal.

With two defenders squaring up to him, he managed to squeeze a shot past them, around the keeper, off the post and into the net.

'It's dramatic, it's delightful, it's Denmark!' screamed commentator John Motson.

Denmark won the match 2-0! They were the champions of Europe!

Captain Lars Olsen collected the trophy, and Peter roared with the rest of the fans when he raised it to the sky. It was the ending nobody had ever predicted.

The Danish players partied long and hard into the early hours of the next morning in celebration. When they arrived back in Denmark the next day, 5,000 fans lined up to cheer them on. Peter remembered the feeling that gave him for the rest of his life.

He had helped prove one thing to the world: Denmark was no longer a 'nearly' football nation.

5

THE PREMIERSHIP

In the 1992/1993 season, the Premier League replaced the First Division as the top league in English football. Although back then, it was called the Premiership – not the Premier League.

Football bosses thought the new league was very exciting. They told everybody it was going to start a new era of English football. Nothing would ever be the same again!

For Peter and the rest of the United players, it was pretty much business as usual. They thought the Premiership was basically just the First Division with a new name. But there was one big difference the players instantly noticed.

In the First Division, players had been given football shirts with numbers on the back according to their positions. So whoever was playing in goal got the number 1 shirt, and whoever played as striker got the number 9 shirt. It didn't matter who that player was. Ultimately, it was the position that determined the number of the shirt.

But in the Premiership, players were given their own squad numbers. Their football shirts featured their squad numbers and their surnames on the backs.

It was a big day when the shirts were handed out in the changing rooms.

'Which number did you get?' the players asked one another.

Peter was given the number 1 shirt with *SCHMEICHEL* written on the back. That meant no one else could ever wear the number 1 shirt while he was a Manchester United player. Even if someone else played in goal while Peter was injured, Peter would still be number 1.

It was a small thing, but it was a big visual symbol of how this new league was going to change things.

The other big change was the TV coverage of football games. Football was revamped and repackaged for the home audience, which hugely boosted the popularity of the sport. But for the players, it meant a strange new schedule.

Starting at 4 p.m. on a Sunday was weird, but playing on a Monday night was even weirder. Nobody had ever done that before in the English game!

Peter was ready for anything. He had just won the Euros and now United were trying to win the Premier League. The manager, Alex Ferguson, told them to forget about losing the First Division to Leeds the previous season.

Onwards and upwards!

But five minutes into the new season, Peter had a devastating blow. Sheffield United striker Brian Deane got in between the Reds' defence and scored the first ever goal in the Premier League! It was not the kind of record Peter wanted to be part of.

Manchester United lost that match 2-1, and they lost the following one 3-0. After a draw in their third match, United were bottom of the table. It was a disaster! The team had been hoping to win their first title in twenty-six years, but everything was going wrong.

In November 1992, a rumour began circulating that Manchester United was going to buy Eric Cantona. Cantona was playing for Leeds United at the time, and Peter thought he was a star. Peter had watched Cantona's hat-trick against Liverpool in the 1992 Charity Shield match in amazement.

Let this happen, please let this happen, he thought when he heard the rumours.

People said Cantona was a bit of a wild man.

He had played with half a dozen clubs in France before coming to Leeds. And why else would Leeds be selling such an excellent player if he wasn't also a troublemaker?

But Ferguson saw Cantona as the answer to Manchester United's problems and quickly signed him up. The first time Cantona walked into the United changing room, Peter was surprised to find out that he was shy and a little awkward.

Cantona didn't say much, but his football did all his talking for him.

He took training seriously, even spending time alone before and after training to work on his skills. The other players were inspired by him ... and it started to show in their results.

Manchester United won four games in a row at the end of November and the start of December. They only lost two other games for the rest of the season and were clear at the top of the table in May 1993.

Two games remained.

Aston Villa were in second place and had to beat Oldham Athletic to have any chance of catching United.

The Reds weren't playing until the next day, so Peter did what he always did after training ... He went to sleep.

When he woke up, he checked the Aston Villa score.

They had lost 1-0 to Oldham.

Manchester United had won the league while Peter was sleeping!

Peter rushed out of the house. His neighbour was Steve Bruce, the Manchester United captain. Bruce ran out of his house too, and the pair celebrated together. Then the rest of the team suddenly started arriving from all over Manchester. To celebrate, they had a massive party at Bruce's place!

Ferguson gave a rousing team talk before their match the next day. 'We are the champions now,' he said. 'Go out and prove it!'

They proved it in style, winning the last two games of the season. They topped the table with eighty-four points – ten points ahead of Aston Villa in second place!

For Peter, it had been a wonderful season of football. The opposition had failed to score against United in twenty-two league matches. This achievement earned Peter the nickname 'Mr Clean Sheet'!

The players received their trophy at Selhurst Park after beating Wimbledon on the final day of the season. That's when Peter noticed another big difference between the First Division and the new Premiership. Instead of medals, each player received a mini trophy.

Woah, this really has changed! Peter thought.

6

DOUBLE TROUBLE

Football fans got used to the sight of Peter making incredible saves. He became especially famous for the way he played because he was unlike any other keeper in the league.

His 'starfish' save was his most well-known move. This involved Peter rushing out at attacking players and making himself as big as possible to stop them from scoring. He spread his arms and legs wide and jumped into the air. He looked like a star – hence the name of the save!

Peter got the inspiration for this move from his early days in Denmark. He was a big fan of playing handball before he moved to United. In handball, the opposition threw balls at the keeper as hard as they could from very close range. The keepers had no chance of catching

the ball, so they did everything they could with their bodies to block it. Peter used the same technique when he was in goal for United!

Handball also helped Peter develop his monster throws. Peter could throw the ball over the halfway line! It was a major weapon in the Manchester United arsenal because Peter could turn defence into attack with one of his amazing, dagger-like throws.

The fans were blown away the first time he unleashed one of his massive throws. It happened on the 15th of August 1992 against Sheffield United. Peter's throw was so accurate that he got an assist when United scored at the other end. Wingers such as Ryan Giggs or Andrei Kanchelskis loved knowing that their goalkeeper could put them into attack at the throw of a ball!

United's second season in the Premier League also introduced fans to the sight of Peter in the opposition's penalty area! In a Boxing Day match against Blackburn Rovers, Peter joined the attack when United won a corner in the dying minutes of the game. United were 1-0 down and couldn't afford to lose.

Ferguson shook his head in amazement when he saw Peter striding up the pitch. The other players were equally confused – and that's exactly what Peter wanted.

His presence caused so much chaos that Blackburn took their eye off the ball and United's Paul Ince managed to get the equaliser!

Peter's training in handball and his obsessiveness in keeping fit made him incredibly agile for a man as big as he is. He made some saves that even his coaches couldn't explain. People still talk about the time he scooped away an almost certain goal against Rapid Vienna in the group stage of the 1996/1997 Champions League.

Above all, though, Peter was known for being loud. He continued to scream at his players during matches to keep himself focussed on the game, which led many people to believe Peter was a bad-tempered man

on *and* off the pitch. While this wasn't strictly true, Peter didn't always choose his words carefully.

Peter used to 'help' Gary Neville practise crossing the ball when Neville was coming up in the side. Neville was terrified to get even one ball wrong.

'What's he training with us for?' Peter said when Neville messed up. 'He's rubbish!'

Another of the young lads, Nicky Butt, almost got into terrible trouble with Peter when he accidentally burnt Peter with a scalding hot kettle. Peter certainly wasn't impressed by this!

'I'm going to kill you!' Peter screamed as he chased after Butt.

But there were two serious moments when Peter was almost kicked off the United team altogether.

In January 1994, United played a thrilling game against Liverpool at Anfield. Well, it was thrilling for the fans anyway! The Red Devils went 0-3 up and seemed to be cruising to a victory. But then they took their foot off the pedal and allowed Liverpool to get back into the game. The final result was 3-3.

After most matches, Ferguson didn't spend much time going over the result or the performance. He usually just said, 'Go and get your bath, see you Monday.'

But he wasn't happy after this Liverpool game. Ferguson was screaming and shouting at everybody. In football, this is known as the 'hairdryer treatment' – because the players on the receiving end of these verbal attacks feel like they've been blasted with a hairdryer!

Ferguson focussed most of his anger on Peter. 'Your goal kicks kept landing on the heads of Liverpool defenders!' he shouted.

Normally, the players put their heads down and waited for the shouting to stop. But this time, Peter got mad at Ferguson. It wasn't fair that the team's manager was picking on him!

'You're slipping!' screamed Ferguson.

'So are you!' retorted Peter.

The other players couldn't believe what they were hearing.

The fight raged on, with Ferguson

saying nasty things about Peter, and Peter pointing out other players who hadn't played as well.

Afterwards, Peter was so cross he called his agent. 'Find me a new club,' he said.

But Ferguson was already one step ahead of him. He was not the kind of manager who put up with being disrespected by his players in front of other people. He called Peter into his office and fired him!

Peter said he was sorry, and Ferguson accepted his apology.

'But it doesn't alter the fact you will have to leave,' Ferguson said.

Peter only saved his skin after he gathered the squad around and apologised for his behaviour. Ferguson secretly heard the sincere apology and never spoke of the firing again.

At least that fight remained verbal. Peter's conflict with Roy Keane actually came to blows. It happened one night during a pre-season tour of South Asia.

Keane and Butt came back late to the hotel and bumped into Peter in reception. There was a bit of banter back and forth, but Peter didn't find it funny. There had been growing tension between him and Keane for quite some time.

'I've had enough of you,' Peter told Keane. 'It's time we sorted this out.'

'Okay,' said Keane.

The pair fought, with Butt acting as a referee. Peter ended up with a black eye and Keane hurt his hand.

'I just got an elbow at training,' Peter told the press when they asked about the damage.

Peter and Keane made up after that. The fight released any tension between them and strengthened their partnership.

None of this nonsense off the pitch affected the team's performance in the second season of the Premier League. The Reds went top of the league after just four matches, and they were still there at the end of the season. They won the league for the second year in a row, and they also added the FA Cup to their trophy cabinet!

The only thing that stopped United from winning a domestic treble was a 3-1 loss to Aston Villa in the final of the League Cup.

The message was clear: United was a force to be reckoned with in English football.

But that wasn't good enough for Ferguson or Peter.

They set their sights on the one trophy they'd yet to win in this new era: the UEFA Champions League.

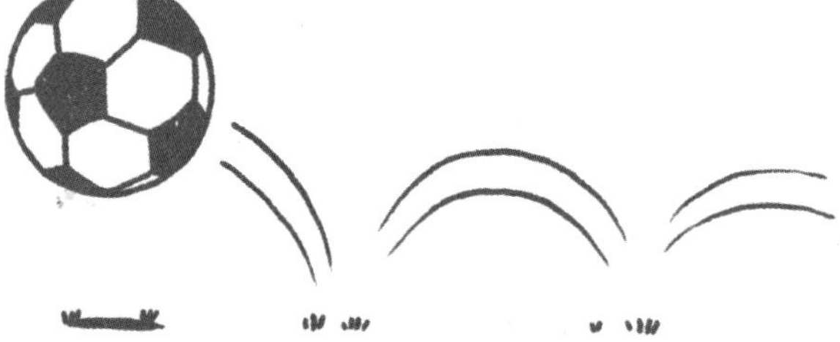

7

HISTORY MAKER

Manchester United won the double again in 1995/1996, and then they claimed the Premier League title for the fourth time in five years in the 1996/1997 season. But they still couldn't get a foothold in the Champions League.

Their first attempt in 1993 ended in a disappointing defeat to Turkish club Galatasaray. In the first leg, which was a 3-3 draw, Peter caused a scandal when a pitch invader got too close to him. He tackled the Galatasaray supporter to the ground, dragged him off the pitch and then threw him over the touchline.

When United went to Turkey for the second leg, it seemed like everybody in the country wanted to get their own back on the team because of what Peter had done.

It was even worse when the players had to go to the stadium.

Police surrounded the players and barked orders at them in an incredibly scary way. The fans put up signs that read, *WELCOME TO HELL!* and *THIS IS THE END OF THE ROAD*. There were fights before, during and after the match. It was a nightmare, and United went out of the competition after losing the tie.

The team managed to reach the semi-final in the 1996/1997 season, but they missed out on the championship altogether the year afterwards.

By this point, Peter had been with the club since 1991. He was soon going to turn thirty-five years old. He hated to admit it, but he was starting to feel old.

'I need more time between games than I can get in England,' Peter said. 'I need to train more than I have ever had to in order to prepare myself properly – and I certainly need more than twelve days' summer holiday.'

He decided that the 1998/1999 season was going to be his last chance for European glory with United.

Peter was going to leave the Reds at the end of the season. 'I have had a fantastic career with United and I owe it to the club, players and fans to do everything I can to finish on a successful note,' he said.

But United started the season slowly. In December, the team put in a terrible display against Middlesborough that ended in a 3-2 defeat.

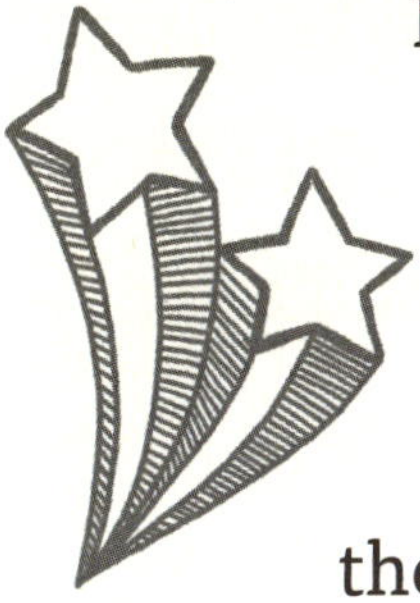

'How did we play so badly?' the players asked themselves after the game. They talked it out and decided that they had to get better. They weren't winning enough.

'Let's just agree between us not to lose another game,' they said.

'Thirty-one wins, and we'll have an unbelievable season!' someone joked.

The players laughed ... but it started a routine that they stuck to for the rest of the season.

After the next game, Dwight Yorke ticked off an imaginary list. 'Thirty wins, boys!' he said.

Two games later, he exclaimed, 'Twenty-eight wins!'

At the end of January, United went to Charlton Athletic on a cold, gloomy day. They were third in the league and needed a win. But Charlton was tough and disciplined, and their pitch wasn't in the best condition. The game looked like it was going to be a miserable 0-0.

It was an especially hard game for Peter. He dislocated his finger and needed a doctor to pop it back into place. Peter soon dislocated the finger again and called for the doctor a second time. The doctor then put a bandage on his hand to stop it from happening again.

United kept pushing and searching for answers until, in the last minute of normal time, Paul Scholes crossed to Yorke, who dinked the ball into the net with his head.

It wasn't pretty and it wasn't fun, but United found the win. They battled to the very last minute in every game and ground out the victory if they had to.

In the changing room after the match, Yorke smiled and said, 'Hey, boys … twenty-four wins!'

Peter got his starring moment in the semi-final of the FA Cup against Arsenal. Even though the game was full of excitement and drama, neither team could find a goal. But then Arsenal won a penalty in stoppage time ...

The Gunners' penalty taker was Dennis Bergkamp. He was a legend for Arsenal and up there amongst the very best forwards of his time.

But Peter didn't care about any of that. If someone was taking a penalty against him, they were entering his world. He treated the penalty takers as if they were nothing to him.

He decided which way he was going to dive and threw himself in that direction the moment Bergkamp hit the ball.

He guessed right.

The ball came to him at the perfect height, and he pushed it aside with ease.

When the match finished, the scoreline was still 0-0. There were no penalty shoot-outs in the FA Cup at the time, so the winner had to be decided by a replay. This meant that United and Arsenal had to play the match again just a few days later. United won 2-1!

'Hey, boys ... ten more wins!' said Yorke.

Peter's favourite save of the season came against Inter Milan in the Champions League. It was the first leg of the quarter-final.

Fabio Galante found some space on United's right and lifted a perfect cross into the United box. Iván Zamorano got behind the United defence and dived at the header. Everybody in the

stadium assumed it was a goal …

Everybody except Peter.

Peter bolted across his line and jumped in his famous starfish style. He kept his eyes on the ball and his wrists strong. He cuffed the ball away, leaving Inter wondering just what they had to do to beat this man mountain.

United won the match 2-0.

On the 16th of May 1999, United completed their Premier League victory with a 2-1 win against Tottenham Hotspur. They beat second-placed Arsenal by one point.

On the 22nd of May 1999, United clinched the double with an FA Cup final win over Newcastle United.

That meant two-thirds of their ultimate goal of thirty-one wins was complete.

All that was left was the UEFA Champions League final. It would be Peter's last game in a United shirt.

No English team had ever done the treble before. Could Manchester United be the first?

8

CHAMPIONS LEAGUE FINAL

'There isn't a team in the world who play as well as you do,' Alex Ferguson told his players before the Champions League final. 'And that's why you mustn't be afraid. There's no reason to be. No team can beat you if you play at the level you are capable of – and of course, that's what you'll do.'

Peter remembered those words as Mehmet Scholl's ball hit the post and rebounded into his arms.

It was a miracle.

We are not going to concede any more goals, Peter thought. He knew it with absolute certainty.

And that belief began to spread throughout the team.

United had eleven minutes to play.

They might never get another chance to win the Champions League, let alone the treble.

It was now or never.

United started to throw more players upfield and attack the Bayern goal more often. Ole Gunnar Solskjær came off the bench to refresh the strikers on the pitch. Peter liked what he saw in Solskjær's determined face and confident run.

Peter sprinted to take every goal kick. He got the ball back to his outfield players as quickly as he could. Every second counted. They had to throw everything they had at this Bayern side.

Solskjær made a good header moments later, forcing the Bayern keeper into a save. Yorke went close. Teddy Sheringham mishit a shot. Neville pushed higher and higher up the pitch. David Beckham delivered countless crosses.

United's focus on attack gave Bayern chances, too. They broke towards goal numerous times. They even hit the bar in the 84th minute. But they couldn't get it past the great Dane between the United posts.

Peter felt invincible. *Come and*

shoot, he thought, *because you'll just be giving us back the ball.*

Yet the clock ticked mercilessly towards ninety minutes.

Then the fourth official was putting up his board. The game was entering stoppage time. There were three minutes left to play.

Neville got the ball on the left of the Bayern box. He attempted a cross, but the Bayern defence cleared it out for the corner.

Peter took a chance of his own. He ran into the Bayern box and waited for Beckham to deliver the corner.

He looked at the Bayern defenders and thought, *You've dealt with everything, but let's see if you can deal with me.*

Beckham floated the ball towards Peter. Peter jumped too early and the ball grazed his head, but his plan worked. The Bayern defence were confused by this blond giant in a green goalkeeper's kit in their box. Three players tried to defend him.

The ball flicked past them to an unmarked United player: Dwight Yorke.

Yorke headed the ball back towards the area.

A Bayern player, Michael Tarnat, half-cleared it away.

Ryan Giggs volleyed it back towards the area.

Teddy Sheringham was now unmarked in the box. The ball fell to him, so he clipped it towards the goal.

Goal! It was 1-1!

Manchester United had scored in the 91st minute!

There was pandemonium all around the stadium. The United players cheered and screamed. The Bayern players slumped in disbelief.

Peter rushed back to his goal.

He suddenly felt very nervous.

It's extra time, he thought. *Golden goal. I cannot be the one to make a mistake and give it away.*

Bayern restarted the match, but United got the ball back almost immediately. They hoofed it downfield to Solskjær, and he won another corner.

'You have to feel this is their year,' said the commentator. 'Is this their moment?'

Peter didn't go into the box this time. He didn't want to give any opportunity for Bayern to sneak a last-minute victory with an open goal.

He watched as Beckham curled the corner in again.

Sheringham got a flick on at the near post.

Solskjær poked out a foot.

Goal!

It was 2-1 in the 93rd minute. There were seconds left to play!

The Bayern players were stunned. Some of them fell to the floor in exhaustion and tears.

Solskjær ran away celebrating. The United players jumped all over him.

Ferguson and his staff hugged and jumped and punched the air.

Peter did a cartwheel.

There were amazing scenes all around the Nou Camp.

But there was still some time left to play. Bayern prepared to kick off one last time.

Peter couldn't get rid of his nerves. His heart was racing.

Don't shoot, he pleaded with the Bayern players in his head. *Don't shoot. I'm in no state to save the ball.*

Then, almost immediately, the referee blew the final whistle.

They'd done it! Manchester United had won the treble!

What just happened? Peter thought.

United fans, players and staff went crazy.

Peter jumped on Teddy Sheringham in celebration. He lifted Raimond van der Gouw into the air. He was in a daze. His last game for United and this was how it ended!

His final act as a Manchester United player was putting his hands on the

UEFA Champions League trophy. He held one handle while Ferguson held the other. They both kissed it and then raised it to the sky.

The crowd went wild.

The players went wild.

Everybody went wild!

'Not even Hans Christian Andersen could have written a fairy tale like that,' said Peter.

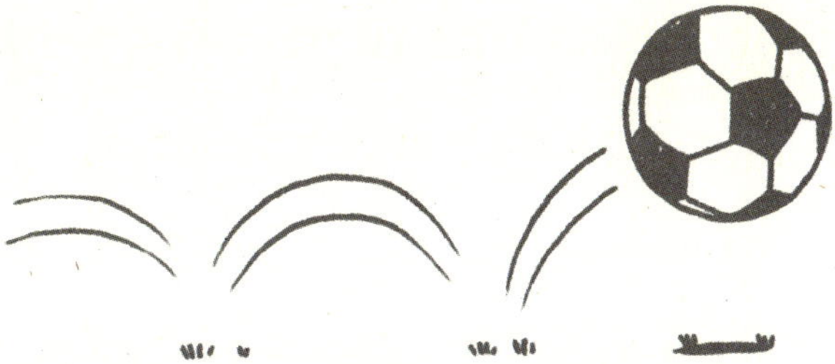

9

(NOT QUITE) THE END

The first thing Peter did after finishing his United career was take a holiday.

He took his wife and kids to Barbados and tried to stay away from everything for a couple of glorious weeks. It was the first time he'd been on holiday in three years.

Peter played the next season with Sporting Lisbon in Portugal. It was a successful season, with Sporting winning the league.

But Peter wasn't happy.

Neither was Manchester United.

Ferguson struggled to fill the large hole Peter had left in the United defence. He wanted Peter to come back to Manchester. Peter wanted to come back to Manchester.

'It's too late in the day for me to get used to the Portuguese system,' Peter told the Sporting bosses. 'I'm thirty-six. I want to live as normal a life as possible, and I want to return to England.'

But then Ferguson stopped answering his phone. And when he finally answered it again, Peter didn't like what he heard.

'I have to think about the future of the club,' Ferguson said.

The deal was off.

Ferguson signed the goalkeeper Fabien Barthez instead.

Peter wasn't going to go back to United, but he did eventually return to England.

In the 2001/2002 season, Peter played for Aston Villa in the Premier League. He earned another European trophy with the club, taking home the UEFA Intertoto Cup.

Peter's greatest achievement at Villa came in a game against Everton in October 2001.

In the final minutes of the game, Peter ran into the Everton box. The ball whipped in towards him, taking a flick from one of the players along the way. It looped into the air, and Peter caught it perfectly in a volley.

Goal!

Peter was the first goalkeeper ever to score in a Premier League match! It was the eleventh goal of his career – not bad for a goalkeeper!

The final club Peter played for was a shock to everybody in the footballing world. He returned to Manchester ... but signed for Manchester City!

Gary Neville was so upset with Peter about this 'betrayal' that he refused to shake hands with Peter when Manchester City played

Manchester United that season. But Peter didn't mind, especially because Manchester City didn't lose to Manchester United. In fact, Peter ended his career never having lost a Manchester derby!

His final game of professional football was in May 2003.

'My body is not happy anymore,' Peter said. 'I always promised I'd move on when this moment arrived. It's time to end my playing career.'

He had to make way for the next generation ... including someone very close to his heart.

10

PETER'S LEGACY

In 2014, Peter was back at Old Trafford – but this time he was only watching a match. He was in one of the boxes, and he was sitting with his son, Kasper. As they were enjoying the game, somebody brought around the Premier League trophy so that the guests could take pictures with it. When the trophy made its way to Peter and Kasper, they posed for a photo.

'The next time I hold this trophy it will be because I've won it,' Kasper said. 'Next time you see my picture with it will be when it is mine.'

Kasper had become a professional goalkeeper just like his father. He'd been playing the game for as long as he could remember. It was hard not to when you grew up in the shadow of Old Trafford! But Kasper hadn't always wanted to be a footballer.

He only started taking the game seriously when the family moved to Portugal while Peter was playing for Sporting Lisbon. From that point onwards, Kasper never looked back. But it wasn't always easy following in the footsteps of someone people think of as the greatest goalkeeper in the world.

As a child, Kasper got plenty of stick from kids and their parents about being a Schmeichel. 'Hah, you think you're as good as your dad,' they yelled, 'but you're rubbish!'

The insults hurt Kasper's feelings, of course. Peter tried to comfort him. 'This is part of it,' Peter told him. 'If you want to play football, you have to take this stuff.'

At first, Kasper thought, *If this is football, I want no part of it*. He quit his team and joined a gymnastics squad instead.

Kasper eventually found his way back to football, and he put his gymnastics training to good use between the goalposts. He joined the Manchester City youth setup when Peter signed for the first team.

But even as Kasper climbed through the ranks of his sport, people still compared him to his father. One time, Kasper and Peter were enjoying a round of golf when an old man approached them.

'Mr Schmeichel, I've been watching you all my life and you are the best goalkeeper I've ever seen,' he said. 'I am a big Manchester United fan.'

Then he said to Kasper, 'And you, young man. You're not bad either. In fact, you're very good. But you will never be as good as your dad.'

That drove Peter crazy! 'Why are you talking like that?' he told the old man. 'How's that going to help?'

Kasper tried not to let the comparisons get him, and after a while, he learnt to live with it. Besides, he was busy making a name for himself.

After taking that picture with the Premier League trophy with Peter in 2014, Kasper won a promotion to the Premier League with his club, Leicester City. Then in the 2015/2016 season, Leicester City

achieved the seemingly impossible to claim the title for themselves. Kasper's prediction that day with his father came true!

Peter and Kasper are still the only father and son pair to have both won the Premier League title. But Peter has changed the beautiful game in more ways than that.

It was Peter more than anybody who influenced the way goalkeepers

play today and how they are treated by their clubs. Peter pushed Manchester United to include him in their training and tactics and make their keeper an all-round playmaker.

His style of pushing and controlling his defence was revolutionary. Not to mention the way he rushed out to charge down one-on-one attacks – and his incredible starfish jumps. It's now also a common sight to see goalies rushing up to attack during last-minute corners. But nobody had ever thought to do it before Peter came along.

They called him the Great Dane during his peak playing years, and he left behind a great legacy. No discussion about the greatest goalkeeper of all time is complete without the name Peter Schmeichel.